ALIEN ALLURE

"NASA's Deep Dive Into UFOs, Independent Study Report and Next Generation Insights with AI and ML"

ERIC DAWSON

Eric Dawson

TABLE OF CONTENTS

INTRODUCTION

CHAPTER ONE

A SHORT REVIEW OF UFO CASES

BUT WHAT PRECISELY IS GOING ON IN THE SKY THAT IS ODD?

CHAPTER TWO

TECHNIQUES FOR ASSESSMENT AND SOURCES OF DATA

WHICH IS NECESSARY TO TELL THE UAP'S HISTORY?

WHAT UAP INDICATIONS ARE MISTAKEN IN NON-PROFIT AND CORPORATE DATA?

"EXTENDING NASA'S DATA HORIZONS FOR UAP INSIGHTS"

CHAPTER THREE

RESTRICTIONS AND ANALYTIC TECHNIQUES

"UNCHARTED SCIENTIFIC FRONTIERS: EXAMINING THE HISTORY AND PROSPECTS OF UAP"

EXPLORE UAP: ANALYSING MYSTERIOUS SOURCES USING PHYSICAL CONSTRAINTS"

CHAPTER FOUR

ACCESSIBLE GOVERNMENT DATA: The Mysterious Trace of Unidentified Aerial Products in Airspace for Civil Aviation"

UPDATING DATA SYSTEMS FOR ILL-FOUND ENCOUNTERS

BOOSTING FUTURE ATM DEVELOPMENT FOR BETTER UAP UNDERSTANDING

CHAPTER FIVE

Eric Dawson

PROMINENT UAP RESEARCHERS, SUCH AS BILL NELSON AND DR. NICOLA FOX, ARE INTERVIEWED AND GIVEN OPINIONS

BILL NELSON

NICOLA FOX DISCUSSES NASA'S UAP RESEARCH AND SCIENTIFIC INTEGRITY.

DAVID SPERGEL, CHAIRMAN OF THE UAP INDEPENDENT RESEARCH TEAM AND PRESIDENT OF THE SIMONS FOUNDATION.

DAN EVANS, NASA'S SCIENCE MISSION DIRECTORATE'S ASSISTANT DEPUTY ASSOCIATE ADMINISTRATOR FOR RESEARCH.

CHAPTER SIX

Insights Gained from Our Investigation into Unidentified Aerial Phenomena (UAP)

NASA comments on the well-known "alien" photos from Mexico

The identity of the new UFO boss remains a mystery due to threats.

NASA suggests making use of AI tools.

NASA gathered researchers and scientists to talk about Unexplained Strange Events.

The Pentagon looks into Unexplained Aerial Phenomena, or UAPs for short.

FINALLIES AND GENUINE ADVICE FROM NASA

INDIVIDUALS IN THE NASA UNIDENTIFIED ABNORMAL PHENOMENON INDEPENDENT STUDY TEAM

Eric Dawson

INTRODUCTION

In recent years, a number of credible witnesses—often military pilots—have reported seeing unexplained flying objects over US airspace. Only a small portion of these occurrences can be immediately classified as either natural or man-made phenomena, despite the fact that the majority of them have already been explained. All of these occurrences are referred to as UAP1, or Unidentified Anomalous Phenomena.

The comprehensive scientific method-based exploration of the unknown is at the heart of NASA's mission. This entails questioning our presumptions and instincts, transparently and methodically obtaining data, validating the findings, obtaining outside assessment, and ultimately coming to a consensus among scientists about the

Eric Dawson

nature of an event. In order to draw conclusions, the scientific method compels us to look past our preconceived assumptions, be open to being proven incorrect, and pay attention to the evidence.

NASA asserts that in addition to a change in public perception of unexplained flying objects, new scientific methods—such as the use of sophisticated satellites—will be required for the study of UFOs.

The negative perception of UFOs is a hindrance to data collection, as highlighted by an independent team NASA hired in a 33-page analysis. The association between unexplained abnormal occurrences, or UAPs, and stigma should be reduced, according to officials, with NASA's assistance.

More directly linked to well-known events or phenomena are the majority of UAP sightings. An instance of this problem can be found in eyewitness accounts, which, while fascinating and compelling in and of themselves, are rarely replicable and

Eric Dawson

typically do not provide enough details to allow for any conclusive judgements to be made about the sources of UAPs. The absence of data necessary to explain these anomalous observations is our main barrier to further research on such events. Therefore, comprehending UAP necessitates a solid, data-driven, scientific framework built on empirical research.

This book contains a report that is broken up into chapters that contain the questions and answers related to the task statement. The study is reviewed in the chapters. It was conducted by a group of sixteen scientists who worked independently. There were also experts in data science, AI, and aviation safety in attendance.
The study's goal was to give NASA a blueprint for collecting and evaluating information about these occurrences in a way that is even more scientific.

This book explains NASA's strategy, potential research contributions, and how the agency's efforts will support broader government initiatives to comprehend UAP.

Eric Dawson

CHAPTER ONE

A SHORT REVIEW OF UFO CASES

BUT WHAT PRECISELY IS GOING ON IN THE SKY THAT IS ODD?

The US may have discovered the wreckage of an extraterrestrial spaceship, according to a whistleblower, which has led to a surge in interest in unidentified flying objects.

In June, the House Oversight Committee announced that it would hold a hearing on "Unidentified Aerial Phenomena," or UFOS, as the U.S. government calls them. Congress was unsatisfied even after the Pentagon denied the report. A spokesperson for the committee stated, "Reports continue to surface regarding unidentified anomalous phenomena in addition to recent claims by a whistleblower."

Eric Dawson

Such reports have been around for many years. After World War II, there was an abrupt increase in unexplained reports, which signalled the start of the modern era of UFO sightings and investigations.

1947–1969: Blue Book Project

Over a two-decade period, the U.S. Air Force documented 12,618 sightings of UFOs as part of what is now known as Project Blue Book. These include objects, lights, and unexplained radar readings that have been observed by weather observers, astronomers, military, and private pilots, among other people.

The project was abandoned in 1969 when a University of Colorado study concluded that there was no evidence of extraterrestrial life and that most sightings might have been the product of frauds or natural occurrences. "Our general conclusion is that nothing has come from the study of UFOs in the past 21 years that has added to scientific knowledge," says research chief Edward U.

Eric Dawson

Condon. Additional research, in his words, "cannot be justified."

Still, sightings and rumours persisted, frequently to the dismay of the original investigators. The Air Force stated in a 1985 information sheet that Wright-Patterson Air Force Base, the site of the investigation, "is not home to, nor has it ever has, any extraterrestrial visitors or equipment."

1995: A U.S. Senator expresses curiosity

The Condon study did not quell public curiosity about UFOs. For the next few decades, so-called "UFOlogists" bombarded government agencies with open records requests in an attempt to get more information about the encounters.

(The legend surrounding Area 51 and the reasons it intrigues us.)

The National Institute for Discovery Science is a small organisation that businessman Robert Bigelow founded in 1995 to investigate the possibility of extraterrestrial life. Participants

Eric Dawson

included current U.S. Senator Harry Reid, a Democrat from Nevada, and two former astronauts, Ed Mitchell and Harrison Schmitt.

Reid subsequently said, "A lot of people said it would ruin my career." That didn't exactly work out that way, however, since Reid went on to play a significant role in spearheading the US government's UFO probe.

2004: A meeting in San Diego

In November 2004, while on a training trip, two Navy pilots got a mission to intercept a mysterious aircraft. They saw and were able to capture on camera an unusual, oval-shaped UFO that was about forty feet long and hovering over the Pacific Ocean a hundred miles off the coast of San Diego. It shot off before the pilots could get close. One of the pilots at the time, Cmdr. David Fravor, stated, "I have no idea what I saw." "It outran our F-18s despite lacking rotors, wings, or plumes."

Eric Dawson

2007: A fresh probe by the Pentagon

Reid, the majority leader of the U.S. Senate, supported the Pentagon's launch of the Advanced Aerospace Threat Identification Programme to investigate the most recent wave of sightings.

The CIA declared in briefing papers that "what was once considered science fiction is now science fact." The project was overseen by military intelligence officer Luis Elizondo, who worked closely with Bigelow's aeronautical research organisation.

2014: An East Coast near-collision

Around Florida and Virginia during this time, Navy pilots reported several encounters with unidentified craft that were capable of reaching high altitudes and hypersonic speeds. The pilots also captured the encounters on film. A pilot reported a near-collision in 2014. A second later told 60 Minutes that characterising the craft was challenging. "You are at high altitudes and you have rotation." Do you have

Eric Dawson

propulsion, I take it? I'm not certain. To be honest, I'm not sure what it is.

One path to take? surveillance ship built overseas.

2017: Public release

These incidents and investigations were mostly kept under wraps until December 2017, when the New York Times disclosed the existence of the Pentagon's Advanced Aerospace Threat Identification Programme. Although Pentagon authorities claimed the programme had ended in 2012, Elizondo told the publication he continued its informal work until his departure in the autumn of 2017. In this endeavour, he received support from the CIA and the Navy.

That sparked a renewed interest in UFOs among the general public, the media, and even scientists.

2020: An appeal from science

In a July 2020 Scientific American article, NASA scientists Ravi Kopparapu and Jacob

Eric Dawson

Haqq-Misra—who specialise in astrobiology and science, respectively—argued that it was time to reexamine the conclusions of the Condon report. They continued, "Perhaps some, or even most, UAP events are just weird weather formations, classified military aircraft, or other misidentified mundane phenomena." "Yet, there are still a number of genuinely perplexing cases that merit further examination."

(This is where Earthling visitors might search for extraterrestrial life.)

With the intention of "improving its understanding of, and gaining insight into, the nature and origins" of the unexplained objects, the Pentagon formed the Unidentified Aerial Phenomena Task Force in August 2020.

2021: Report on DNI

In April 2021, the Navy confirmed footage of mysterious objects "buzzing" US warships near California. The incident would be added to the list

Eric Dawson

of sightings that have been reported for additional investigation.

June saw the release of the "preliminary assessment" by the Office of the Director of National Intelligence (DNI) regarding incidents of unidentified flying objects that occurred between 2004 and 2021. The paper states that the UFOs, which are now known as UAPs, can be categorised into five different categories: natural atmospheric phenomena, airborne clutter, public and commercial aerospace developmental programmes, foreign enemy systems, and "a catchall 'other' bin." The report suggested increasing funding and reporting.

NASA launches an investigation in 2022.

The Pentagon created the All-domain Anomaly Resolution Office in April 2022 with the intention of investigating objects "that might pose a threat to national security."

In June of that year, NASA announced that it was setting up a separate research programme to tackle

Eric Dawson

the issue from a scientific perspective. "We will be identifying what data—from civilians, government, nonprofits, and companies—exists, what else we should try to collect, and how to best analyse it," stated David Spergel, the head of the research team. The term "Unidentified Aerial Phenomena" was changed once more to "Unidentified Anomalous Phenomena" in official usage in 2022.

2023, perhaps? There's still more to discover: Report of the Independent Study Team

Nothing about what's going on above has been fully clarified yet. In a follow-up report published in June 2023, the DNI listed 510 further sightings, 171 of which were still unsolved. According to the study, in similar situations, unidentifiable planes often "appear to have demonstrated unusual flight characteristics or performance capabilities."

The most shocking claim was made by a former intelligence officer called David Grusch in a

Eric Dawson

whistleblower report that was published in June. Grusch said that the U.S. government had "intact and partially intact vehicles" from UFO crash sites. He said that the vessels were "non-human" in origin. However, he also acknowledged that he had never seen the artefacts himself, which prompted doubt from other specialists.

The independent study team, set up outside of NASA, used unclassified data from civilian government entities, commercial data, and data from other sources to inform their findings and recommendations in the report.

There are currently a limited number of high-quality observations of UAP, which currently make it impossible to draw firm scientific conclusions about their nature.

The team's report contains the findings and recommendations which aim to inform NASA on what possible data is available to be collected and how the agency can help shed light on the origin and nature of future UAP.

Eric Dawson

CHAPTER TWO

TECHNIQUES FOR ASSESSMENT AND SOURCES OF DATA

WHICH IS NECESSARY TO TELL THE UAP'S HISTORY?

"What kinds of scientific data that NASA and other civilian government agencies currently collect and maintain need to be combined and analysed in order to potentially provide light on the composition and origins of Unidentified Anomalous Phenomena (UAP)?"

To help with the difficulties of locating and/or comprehending UAP, NASA maintains a sizable library of past and present data sets in addition to a wide range of planned and operational Earth and space observational assets. The majority of data pertaining to Earth observation is gathered by

Eric Dawson

NASA's satellite network. However, they frequently lack the spatial resolution required to find objects as small as UAP.

They still have a significant supporting role to perform in figuring out which environmental factors are associated with UAP. For example, the advanced sensors on board the Terra and Aqua missions should be used directly to investigate the local earth, ocean, and atmospheric conditions that are contemporaneous in both space and time with UAP that was discovered through alternative means. NASA can therefore assist in ascertaining whether specific environmental factors are associated with documented UAP traits or occurrences.

Other possible civilian roles could be used to look into UAP. Important items must be separated from airborne clutter using tools like the Geostationary Operational Environmental Satellites and the NEXRAD Doppler radar network, which consists of

Eric Dawson

160 weather radars that are jointly maintained by the National Weather Service, the U.S. Air Force, and the FAA. Aside from that, future large-sky surveys made possible by ground-based telescopes such as the Vera C. Rubin Observatory would be extremely helpful in the hunt for anomalous objects outside of the Earth's atmosphere.

Additionally, NASA has a great deal of experience with Synthetic Aperture Radar (SAR), which provides images of the Earth with a much higher angular resolution and can confirm surface motion and change. The panel believes that SAR-based Earth observation satellites have a lot of potential. One such project is the NISAR (NASA-ISRO Synthetic Aperture Radar) project, which is a collaboration with the Indian Space Research Organisation. Significant radar data will be available thanks to NISAR's exceptional resolution, which could be essential for evaluating UAP in relation to their environmental context. Because of their Doppler signals, SAR instruments will be

Eric Dawson

crucial for verifying any highly unusual features, such as rapid acceleration or high-G movements.

It is imperative to recognise the crucial role that systematic data curation plays in comprehending UAP within a rigorous, evidence-based framework, regardless of the source of the observation. Most observations in UAP data currently available were not meant for a systematic scientific analysis; instead, they were initially collected for other reasons, possibly with inadequate metadata. NASA can play a significant role in this because of its unmatched proficiency in the curation, storage, and exchange of large volumes of data.

Scientists and citizen scientists can perform data-mining and intelligent analysis because NASA is dedicated to the FAIR (Findability, Accessibility, Interoperability, and Reusability) data principles while creating curated data repositories. Furthermore, disparities exist in the methods used for data collection, processing, and filtering because

Eric Dawson

there isn't a comprehensive system in place for compiling reports from civilian UAPs. Following NASA's rigorous guidelines for UAP data procedures will ultimately be necessary to gain a complete understanding of these events.

WHAT UAP INDICATIONS ARE MISTAKEN IN NON-PROFIT AND CORPORATE DATA?

"What categories of scientific data are now being gathered and stored by non-profits and businesses that should be combined and examined in order to perhaps give insight on the nature and causes of UAP?"

There is an incredible array of Earth-observing sensors available on the commercial remote sensing market in the United States that can be used to directly address UAP incidents. For example, commercial satellite constellations provide images with sub- to several-meter spatial resolution that precisely match the typical spatial sizes of known

Eric Dawson

UAP. Moreover, commercial remote-sensing networks' high temporal cadence raises the possibility of covering UAP events that were first detected by other means.

We will need to be extremely lucky to obtain such observations for a specific UAP event because commercial satellites do not currently cover a large portion of the Earth's surface with high resolution. As a result, the amount of data available is limited. Beyond this, the panel commends US industry and academic efforts to employ one or more low-cost, ground-based sensors that can scan a significant portion of the sky. These sensors could provide physical clues about UAP, but they might also be crucial for spotting "pattern-of-activity" tendencies. They could be quickly placed anywhere that UAP activity is known to occur.

However, reliable data calibration is required once more, and NASA may be able to offer crucial advice in this area as well. Data accuracy,

Eric Dawson

dependability, and the absence of systematic biases or errors are guaranteed through the calibration of sensors and equipment. Precise calibration is even more important because data from UAP studies frequently come from equipment not intended for finding these things. To properly define the sensor and a potential UAP, metadata that contains contextual information such as sensor type, manufacturer details, noise characteristics, and capture time is also needed.

After careful calibration and metadata analysis, it was discovered that several suspected UAP were actually sensor aberrations. Owing to the standardisation of the data gathered via thoughtful calibration, a thorough scientific assessment of UAP will be possible, despite the high associated costs. NASA has significant experience in this area.

Eric Dawson

"EXTENDING NASA'S DATA HORIZONS FOR UAP INSIGHTS"

"What additional kinds of scientific information might NASA gather to improve its chances of better comprehending the nature and causes of UAP?"

NASA needs to be involved in creating a comprehensive plan for data collection that fits within the larger framework of the entire government in order to enhance our understanding of UAP. Many carefully calibrated sensors are necessary in order to identify UAP. NASA might make use of multispectral or hyperspectral data as part of a comprehensive effort to obtain additional information on likely UAP, given its extensive knowledge in this field. Planned large-sky surveys, made possible by Federal ground-based facilities such as the Vera C. Rubin Observatory, will also yield a wealth of data that could potentially be used

Eric Dawson

in a direct search for anomalous objects outside Earth's atmosphere.

There are a tonne of data signatures, and theories that predict distinct signatures help focus our searches. Clearly defined proof requirements are essential to avoid errors, especially in automated procedures. For better detection, future UAP detection sensors should also be designed with the capacity to change on millisecond timeframes. Transient information should be quickly and universally identified and distributed via alert systems.

The panel notes that it is presently challenging to gather data on UAP due to a lack of sensor information and issues with sensor calibration. Stated differently, gathering data such as the time, place, and sensor observing modes assures a thorough understanding of the contextual and environmental aspects of a recorded UAP event, while calibration guarantees the accuracy and reliability of future data collected. In turn, both will allow for the systematic investigation of UAP occurrences and—more importantly—will enable the elimination of false positives caused by sensor artefacts. In order to improve these variables, future data gathering will need a focused effort. In this situation, NASA's experience should be properly used as part of a robust and rigorous data strategy within the framework of the whole government.

The panel also sees a number of advantages for the present crowdsourcing techniques, such as open-source smartphone apps that complement future data collecting activities by concurrently gathering picture and other sensor data from several citizen observers. Therefore, NASA should investigate the viability of developing or acquiring such a crowdsourcing system as part of a future data strategy.

NASA's network of Earth-observing satellites will play a critical role in future data collecting on

Eric Dawson

environmental conditions linked to UAP sightings, as previously indicated. Despite the disparity in geographical resolution between the present generation of satellites and typical UAP incidences, future satellite data collection and analysis will undoubtedly provide us with insights into the normal environmental characteristics associated with UAP. Future missions, like the NOAA/NASA Geostationary Extended Observations (GeoXO) satellite system, will provide even more dependable data, which is essential for UAP research. NASA also needs to employ sensors that allow it to look further, such air/sea interfaces and deeper ocean depths.

The next stage is to expand the scope of data collection operations from radio and optical astronomy to include the whole solar system in addition to the Earth's atmosphere, with the aim of conducting technosignature searches. Furthermore, massive data repositories on events in Earth's atmosphere are available through near-Earth object (NEO) projects. This is an underutilised source of information that may be used to describe both typical occurrences and anomalies. NASA has to consider incorporating these elements as part of a sound future-data strategy.

Last but not least, NASA's involvement in data gathering in the future will be critical in reducing the stigma associated with UAP reporting, which now probably leads to data loss. The public's long-standing trust in NASA is essential for educating the general public about these occurrences and is necessary for de-stigmatizing UAP reporting and scientific research. By employing open reporting and careful analysis when obtaining future data, NASA may be able to set an example for the public on how to approach a topic like UAP. NASA employs scientific procedures that encourage critical thinking.

CHAPTER THREE

RESTRICTIONS AND ANALYTIC TECHNIQUES

"UNCHARTED SCIENTIFIC FRONTIERS: EXAMINING THE HISTORY AND PROSPECTS OF UAP"

"How can the current state of scientific analytical methodologies be applied to assess the origin and development of UAP? What kinds of methods for analysis must be developed?

In large datasets, machine learning (ML) and artificial intelligence (AI) have shown to be invaluable tools for locating unusual occurrences. To investigate the nature and causes of UAP, these approaches should be utilised in concert with

Eric Dawson

NASA's extensive knowledge and experience, using data from sources like as satellites and radar systems. By comparison, the effectiveness of

For AI and ML to successfully investigate UAP, the data utilised for training and subsequent analysis must be of a high calibre. For UAP analysis, the quality of the data now poses a greater limitation than the accessibility of the methodologies. This means that gathering better-quality data should come before developing cutting-edge analytical techniques.

Neural networks may be trained to recognise departures from the norm if AARO and other institutions, such as NASA, have gathered a large and well chosen collection of baseline data. In astronomy, particle physics, and other fields of study, standard procedures may be adapted for these kinds of investigations, the panel concludes. Two approaches, including UAP, are available for finding irregularities in datasets.

First, a model describing the expected signal qualities is created, and any matches are then sought against this model. In the second technique, we use a model of the background properties and search for deviations from it. The panel further notes that the absence of a consistent definition of the physical characteristics of UAP makes the first option difficult.

But in order to distinguish what is unusual and unknown from what is common and well-known in a given search location, the second approach needs to know about it. AARO has been investigating what "normal" phenomena, such as sun glint or balloons, seem to military sensors in order to get this operation off to a good start. A method for calibrating observations of what is "normal" is necessary before starting to hunt for the aberrant.

A third potential scientific research strategy is cross-referencing the locations and timings of UAP instances that have been reported with NASA's

Eric Dawson

extensive database. If a complete set of UAP reports is released to the public, the panel thinks this is a suitable avenue for more research. NASA will once again be able to play a major role because to its expertise with AI and ML.

To be utilised for any scientific study, including UAP analysis, the data used for AI and ML must be collected according to stringent requirements. Utilising tools that are calibrated and tailored to each unique use case, together with metadata that facilitates contextual comprehension and calibration, is necessary for collecting data. Proper curation and integration of data is also necessary to enable scientific analysis.

Developing a baseline knowledge also requires examining known events using well calibrated instruments. NASA is well positioned to play a significant role in this effort to assess UAP throughout the whole government due to its

Eric Dawson

background in advanced analysis, data management, and calibration.

EXPLORE UAP: ANALYSING MYSTERIOUS SOURCES USING PHYSICAL CONSTRAINTS"

"What fundamental physical limitations might the nature and origins of UAP be subjected to in light of the aforementioned factors?"

Although UAP has been seen, there hasn't been a pattern or consistency in the sightings. our makes it hard to physically restrict them, which makes the strict, empirically supported methods our research presents an effective incentive. Modern platforms, drones, balloons, and aeroplanes are capable of reaching a wide range of velocities and accelerations; as a result, the biggest physical constraints do not apply to exceptional events, but rather to common ones.

Eric Dawson

Deviations from this behaviour, such as any well-characterized observations of velocities and accelerations outside of that range, are scientifically fascinating for the purpose of assessing and analysing UAPs. The panel emphasises how crucial it is to compute distances precisely in order to understand and validate any reported anomalous high-velocity and high-acceleration incidents. The findings of AARO, which show that most UAP have simple causes, lend credence to this idea.

The panel believes that physical limitations on UAP, as well as the spectrum of possible types and sources, are achievable if the whole government framework for comprehending UAP—in which NASA plays a major role—were to adhere to the majority of the previously mentioned actions. Assuming that all unexplained events move at normal accelerations and speeds, then a conventional explanation for these events is most likely correct. If there was compelling evidence of

Eric Dawson

verified anomalous accelerations and velocity, it
may lead to possibly creative explanations for
UAPs.

Eric Dawson

CHAPTER FOUR

PROCEDURES FOR COLLECTING AND REPORTING DATA

ACCESSIBLE GOVERNMENT DATA: The Mysterious Trace of Unidentified Aerial Products in Airspace for Civil Aviation"

What information on UAPs in civilian airspace has been obtained by government organisations and is available for research to: a) support efforts to better understand the nature and origins of UAPs; and b) determine the threat posed by UAPs to the National Air Space (NAS)?

Information on civilian airspace that may be inspected to search for UAP is gathered by the FAA and other government agencies. Data from air traffic control towers and radar systems are included in this dataset.

Eric Dawson

It is essential to bear in mind, however, that not all of these data are suitable or suited for a comprehensive scientific study of UAP. Crucial contextual data in the form of metadata is also often missing. The observations almost often come from inadvertent use of instruments not designed for object identification. While civilian airspace data has been used by AARO to support the investigation of a few individual UAP incidents, it is unlikely that the vast amount of such data will provide a complete picture of the extent, composition, or movement of UAP.

Additionally, the Federal mechanism for reporting civilian UAP is still non-standard. As AARO establishes a systematic framework for military and intelligence community UAP reporting, current FAA rules urge civilians who seek to report UAP to contact their local law enforcement or one or more non-governmental groups. As a result, there are no

Eric Dawson

procedures for curation or verification and the data collection is sparse and ad hoc.

As the country attempts to understand UAP, NASA may once again be of great assistance in this field. Due to its unparalleled expertise in data curation and structure, NASA is in an excellent position to provide advice on the best practises for creating repositories of data pertaining to civilian aviation.

UPDATING DATA SYSTEMS FOR ILL-FOUND ENCOUNTERS

"What current procedures for reporting and data collection that air traffic management (ATM) uses could be modified to obtain additional data on past and present UAPs?"

It is evident to the panel that creating a more comprehensive and well-organized structure and data repository for UAP reporting is essential. This is notably the case for civilian reporting of UAP; as of right now, FAA regulations state that anybody reporting UAP should contact their local law enforcement agency or one or more non-governmental groups; nevertheless, this is not enough information to make an academic determination.

Even while eyewitness stories are sometimes captivating and convincing, they are insufficient in and of themselves to make definitive judgements on UAP. As such, its robust validation within a sound reporting and monitoring framework grounded on deliberately collected data (including the ATM system) may prove to be a useful instrument in understanding UAP.

For deeper integration within an organised, evidence-based framework, NASA's Aviation Safety Reporting System (ASRS), which NASA administers for the FAA, presents an especially appealing option. This system is a private, voluntary, non-punitive reporting system that gathers safety reports from pilots, air traffic

Eric Dawson

controllers, dispatchers, cabin crew, ground operators, maintenance staff, and UAS operators. It provides a unique data source for newly identified UAS safety difficulties. Safety-related incidents, threats, violations, and close calls are all reported to ASRS.

In its 47-year existence, ASRS has received approximately 1,940,000 covert safety reports—more than 100,000 on average each year. Every aspect of aircraft operations is covered in reports. The ASRS initiative is fully funded by the FAA and does not come within NASA's aeronautics activities, despite the fact that NASA employees are engaged and the system is housed at NASA Ames.

NASA should give technical assistance in this situation because, while not designed with UAP gathering in mind, employing this system for commercial pilot UAP reporting would provide an essential database that would be helpful for the government's overall effort to understand UAP.

Eric Dawson

BOOSTING FUTURE ATM DEVELOPMENT FOR BETTER UAP UNDERSTANDING

"In order to aid in the endeavour to better understand the nature and origin of the UAPs, what workable improvements to the next ATM development efforts may be suggested to gather information about upcoming reported UAPs?"

Thanks in large part to NASA's strong collaboration with the FAA and its significant research and development of air traffic management technology, future ATM systems that gather UAP data will be developed with this in mind. Currently, surveillance technology is not designed to recognise strange objects and often lacks connected information. NASA should take on the responsibility of developing these systems, beginning with novel ATM system concepts and ideas that enable these systems to support efforts to better understand UAP.

Eric Dawson

NASA could use its knowledge in passive sensing by studying and exhibiting these techniques. NASA also has to consider the technologies that enable new types of data, such as picture data and maybe multi- or hyperspectral data. NASA could look at whether machine learning algorithms added to ATM systems in the future would enable them to identify and evaluate UAP in real-time. The successful execution of this difficult undertaking would allow for the broad and methodical gathering of UAP data as well as a detailed background characterization.

Once again, NASA would be very helpful in identifying and evaluating cutting-edge safety measures due to its knowledge and experience in these areas.

Eric Dawson

CHAPTER FIVE

PROMINENT UAP RESEARCHERS, SUCH AS BILL NELSON AND DR. NICOLA FOX, ARE INTERVIEWED AND GIVEN OPINIONS

BILL NELSON

NASA commissioned the independent study to gain a better understanding of how the organisation might support ongoing government initiatives to advance the study of sky occurrences that defy scientific explanation as balloons, planes, or well-known natural phenomena. NASA Administrator Bill Nelson addressed the proverbial extraterrestrial elephant in the room.

At the time, he said, "We don't know what these UAP are," even though an independent NASA

Eric Dawson

study team had not discovered any evidence linking them to space.

The space agency, according to Nelson, aims to "shift the conversation about UAP from sensationalism to science."

A former Air Force intelligence officer said in a July congressional hearing that the US was hiding a protracted mission to reverse-engineer extraterrestrial spacecraft. Nelson was questioned about this assertion by another reporter.

"Where is the evidence to support anything he said? Nelson responded.

Nelson said, "Do I think there's life in a universe so big that it's hard for me to understand?" in answer to the question. Personally, I say "yes."

NASA is required by legislation to look for alien life. He said, "We'll let you know what we find."

It is in our DNA at NASA to look into and ask questions about the reasons behind occurrences.

Eric Dawson

NASA Administrator Bill Nelson said, "I want to thank the Independent Investigative Team for their advise on how to do so. In the future, NASA can better study and assess UAP. "Using NASA's experience to work with other agencies to analyse UAP and use artificial intelligence and machine learning to scan the sky for anomalies, the new Director of UAP Research will develop and oversee the implementation of NASA's scientific strategy for UAP research. NASA will execute this duty in full openness for the sake of humankind.

NICOLA FOX DISCUSSES NASA'S UAP RESEARCH AND SCIENTIFIC INTEGRITY.

NASA Science Mission Directorate Associate Administrator for UAP Research and Scientific Integrity.

The Unidentified Anomalies Phenomena (UAP) is one of the greatest mysteries in the world today.

Eric Dawson

There have been reports of objects in our sky that cannot be explained by aeroplanes, balloons, or known natural phenomena, despite the fact that there are few high-quality sightings. Since science's purpose is to investigate the unknown, data is the language that scientists employ to solve the mysteries of our world. We now lack the body of evidence necessary to make solid, scientific conclusions on UAP, despite the abundance of reports and photos, since there aren't any consistent, thorough, and well curated observations.

NASA uses data and scientific equipment to investigate the unknown in the atmosphere and space. NASA formed an outside, independent study team in June 2022 to find out how we may use our open-source data and resources to help shed light on the nature of future UAP. NASA hires independent research teams as a formal part of its scientific process; these teams function similarly to a group of peer reviewers. These groups provide the organisation independent counsel and a greater variety of perspectives from reputable scientific professionals.

A diverse range of areas, including science, technology, data, artificial intelligence, space exploration, aerospace safety, media, and business innovation, are represented among the 16 members of NASA's UAP Independent Study Team. They were tasked with finding the UAP-related data that is currently accessible and writing a report outlining a plan for how NASA may make use of its scientific resources to collect important data in order to evaluate and categorise UAP going forward. This is not a historical examination of UAP cases.

We are appreciative of the UAP Independent research Team members' contributions to the study and to the national advancement of UAP awareness. To assist NASA's Science Mission Directorate's whole-of-government approach to comprehending and resolving UAP incidents, the Department of Defense's All-Domain Anomaly Resolution Office

Eric Dawson

(AARO) is dedicated to keeping an open and transparent channel of communication and resources. We're currently reviewing the report and the team's conclusions and suggestions. NASA is appointing a Director of UAP Research to oversee communications and use the agency's extensive resources and expertise to fully engage the whole government in the UAP initiative. This individual will also ensure that the government's unified UAP effort benefits from the agency's vast analytical capabilities, including its proficiency in data management, machine learning, and artificial intelligence.

The principles of openness, transparency, and scientific integrity are important to NASA and are integral to our business practises. Through the establishment of this independent research group, NASA was able to get vital external perspectives from some of the nation's most eminent experts about the optimal utilisation of our resources to

Eric Dawson

enhance the analysis of UAP data and explore unexplored air and space for the good of all.

DAVID SPERGEL, CHAIRMAN OF THE UAP INDEPENDENT RESEARCH TEAM AND PRESIDENT OF THE SIMONS FOUNDATION.

"Our team's fact-finding, open-communication, and dedication to scientific rigour necessitated the use of unclassified material in order to produce this report for NASA. The team produced the report in line with NASA's principles of openness, transparency, and scientific integrity to help the agency shed light on the nature of future UAP incidents, he said. We found that NASA can assist the government's UAP endeavour by using multiple measurements, meticulous data calibration, and meticulous sensor metadata to provide a complete

Eric Dawson

and reliable data collection for further UAP investigations.

On Thursday, David Spergel, the head of the organization's UAP research team, encouraged individuals to report whatever they witnessed. similarly, "collect high-quality data so we can study it." Spergel was speaking at a meeting where his team had just delivered the long-awaited final report on the data and protocols NASA should use to examine unscheduled flights.

Spergel, an astronomer and head of the Simons Foundation, predicted that most accidents would involve everyday devices like balloons and aeroplanes. As the phrase goes, "If you want to find a needle in a haystack, you better know exactly what hay looks like." This is why NASA is useful when assessing planetary conditions.

There may be a role for NASA in the All-domain Anomaly Resolution Office, or AARO, of the

Eric Dawson

Defence Department, which is in charge of the UAP inquiry, according to the report.

When a reporter questioned Spergel about the two mummified bodies that a UFO researcher presented to Mexico's Congress last week, he responded somewhat grudgingly, claiming that they were 1,000-year-old alien corpses.

"This is something I've only seen on Twitter, so, you know," Spergel said, emphasising the need to provide scientists with access to samples so they may examine them.

Eric Dawson

DAN EVANS, NASA'S SCIENCE MISSION DIRECTORATE'S ASSISTANT DEPUTY ASSOCIATE ADMINISTRATOR FOR RESEARCH.

Contrary to its repeated pledges of transparency, the agency has decided not to reveal the name of its new UAP boss. The study team and other individuals associated with the subject matter were subjected to surveillance and harassment, as was mentioned by the agency.

The crew endured nine months of effort and a truckload of hurtful and critical public discourse. Panellists have been subjected to online abuse by those who reject the validity of any inquiry into unidentified aerial photographs (UAPs) and others who think NASA is covering up more of the UFO story than it wants to.

Eric Dawson

Evans said, "We take the security of the team very seriously." "We're not revealing our director's identify everywhere for this reason, in part. Science needs to be autonomous.

More stunning UAP interpretations did not seem to be losing the public's attention despite NASA officials' sombre mood.

Dan Evans, NASA's Science Mission Directorate's assistant deputy associate administrator for research, states that "We can ensure that our skies remain a safe area for everyone by understanding the nature of UAP." "Data help you move from conjecture and conspiracy to science and sanity," stated the speaker.

Eric Dawson

CHAPTER SIX

Insights Gained from Our Investigation into Unidentified Aerial Phenomena (UAP)

A NASA investigation into hundreds of UFO sightings could not completely rule out the possibility that aliens were responsible for the unexplained phenomena, even though there was no proof of such activity.

This eagerly anticipated report offers no evidence that the truth is concealed.

It did, however, include information about how NASA intends to investigate what it refers to as UAPs (Unidentified Anomalous Phenomena) using artificial intelligence and improved technology.

NASA administrator Bill Nelson announced that the organisation will share data more freely

Eric Dawson

and will also be leading the investigation into possible UAP incidents.

Here are some of the most important conclusions from the 36 pages of highly technical and scientific observations in the report.

There might be aliens, even though there's no proof.

The conclusion that "there is no reason to conclude" that the hundreds of UAP sightings that NASA has investigated are the product of extraterrestrial activity was made clear on the report's last page.However, the report said, "If that's accurate, as we think, then those objects had to pass through our solar system to get here.

Although NASA did not come to a conclusion about the existence of extraterrestrial life, it did acknowledge the possibility of "potential

Eric Dawson

unknown alien technology operating in Earth's atmosphere".

Not enough UAP information

As associate administrator of NASA's Science Mission Directorate Nicola Fox put it, "UAP are one of our planet's greatest mysteries," and this is mainly because there is a dearth of high quality data.

According to Ms. Fox, despite the large number of UAP sighting reports, there is typically insufficient data that "may be used to make definitive scientific conclusions about the nature and origin of UAP."

According to Ms. Fox, the new director of UAP research wants to "establish a robust database for the evaluation of future data".

The filmmaker plans to employ AI and machine learning to gather and evaluate data.

Eric Dawson

NASA comments on the well-known "alien" photos from Mexico

BBC reporter Sam Cabral questioned the NASA panel about a set of purported alien photos that were shown to Mexican authorities earlier this week.

Self-described UFO expert Jaime Maussan brought what he claimed to be two ancient "non-human" alien corpses to a congressional hearing. He states that the bodies and artefacts were found in Cusco, Peru, in 2017 and may be as old as 1,800 years, based on radiocarbon dating.

Experts in the field have voiced serious doubts about the authenticity of the specimens, and Mr Maussan has previously made debunked assertions of extraterrestrial life.

NASA scientist Dr. David said, "Make samples available to the world scientific community and the media."

Eric Dawson

The identity of the new UFO boss remains a mystery due to threats.

Unknown at this time is the identity of the incoming NASA director of UAP research.

Given that NASA has pledged to be more transparent about its UAP research, the details of the position and its pay during Thursday's briefing were oddly evasive.

This could be done, among other reasons, to protect the new director from potential public harassment.

According to NASA's Deputy Associate Administrator for Research, Dr. Daniel Evans, "actual threats" had been made against UAP research panel members.

He stated that NASA takes the security and safety of the team "extremely seriously" in response to the threats, and the organisation chose not to disclose the participants' identities.

Eric Dawson

NASA suggests making use of AI tools.

The report states that artificial intelligence and machine learning are "essential tools" for locating UAPs.

The public is yet another "critical aspect of understanding UAP".

NASA has identified one of its biggest challenges as being the lack of data preventing it from better understanding and identifying UAPs. In order to fill this gap, NASA plans to use crowdsourcing techniques.

This includes additional smartphone metadata from "multiple citizen observers worldwide" as well as "open-source smartphone-based apps".

The report states that there is currently no standardised process in place for the collection and categorization of reports from civilian

Eric Dawson

UAPs, "resulting in sparse and incomplete data".

NASA should play a "prominent role" in the federal government's ongoing investigation of unidentified flying objects, or UFOs.

This is the suggestion made by an outside advisory group that encouraged NASA to use its scientific expertise and its current and planned space and Earth observation equipment to better gather data on what is now widely known as "unidentified anomalous phenomena," or UAP.

"Our objective is to shift the conversation around UAPs from sensationalism to science," says NASA administrator Bill Nelson, a space shuttle pilot and former senator from Florida.

Eric Dawson

NASA gathered researchers and scientists to talk about Unexplained Strange Events.

For instance, the new report points out that although NASA's Earth-observing satellites are unable to detect small objects, they may be able to determine whether particular environmental factors are associated with unusual sightings.

According to the report, planned large-sky surveys using telescopes like the Vera C. Rubin Observatory may search for unusual objects located outside of Earth's atmosphere. Programmes designed to search for near-Earth objects, including potentially hazardous asteroids, also gather a great deal of data regarding phenomena in the vicinity of Earth's atmosphere.

Certain data gaps were noted in the report, such as the absence of a uniform procedure that would enable private pilots to report odd sightings. At the moment,

Eric Dawson

residents are encouraged to get in touch with their local law enforcement or other groups. The report observes that "as a result, the collection of data is sparse, unsystematic, and lacks any curation or vetting protocols," and it suggests that NASA could advise other government agencies on how to gather this kind of data.

The panel also mentioned the possibility of crowdsourcing public observations through smartphone apps, suggesting NASA investigate the feasibility of this form of public participation and data gathering.

"The language of scientists is data," observes NASA's Science Mission Directorate Associate Administrator Nicola Fox, who referred to UAP as "one of our planet's greatest mysteries."

Lastly, the advisors note that NASA could help de-stigmatize the reporting of these sightings so that they can be studied more thoroughly, and the agency

Eric Dawson

has a history of transparency and public trust that could be beneficial to the study of UFOs.

Nelson vowed, "We're going to be open about this," emphasising that the organisation is transparent about its operations and data.

According to David Spergel, president of the Simons Foundation and chair of NASA's UAP independent study team, it is critical for scientists to have a strong foundation based on data and to fully comprehend "normal" conditions and objects in the sky in order to distinguish when something is truly unusual.

"Most events are going to turn out to be conventional things, balloons, aeroplanes, and so on," Spergel says.

He likened the process of seeking out something genuinely unique to trying to find a needle in a haystack without knowing what the "needle" will resemble.

Eric Dawson

"If you want to find something strange in a haystack," says Spergel, "you'd better know exactly what hay looks like."

The Pentagon looks into Unexplained Aerial Phenomena, or UAPs for short.

NASA's mission is to discover the unknown. "We don't know what these UAP are," Nelson stated, emphasising that "the NASA independent study team did not find any evidence that UAP have an extraterrestrial origin."

While NASA hasn't historically given "little green men" much thought, it has actively looked for signs of potential life on other solar system planets and moons as well as beyond.

NASA officials announced the appointment of a director for UAP research to help guide and oversee NASA's efforts, praising the idea of the new report

Eric Dawson

offering a roadmap for the agency's contribution to this field of study.

Initially, NASA refused to disclose the name of the person appointed to that position. Dan Evans, assistant deputy associate administrator for research in NASA's Science Mission Directorate, said that part of their reluctance to reveal the individual's identity was to protect them from intimidation by people with strong feelings regarding unidentified flying objects.

"Some of the threats and the harassment have been beyond the pale, quite frankly, towards some of our panellists," Evans says. "That's in part why we are not splashing the name of our new director out there."
But later in the day, NASA did identify the employee who will take over as the new research director. It's Mark McInerney, who the agency purports to have served as its liaison with the Department of Defence on a few UAP-related matters.

Topics discussed by NASA during its meeting regarding unexplained anomalous phenomena

Eric Dawson

The "vast majority" of reported sightings of objects in the sky that appear to be extraterrestrial can, according to the report, be explained by commonplace airborne objects such as weather balloons, drones, and aeroplanes.

Not all, though, are readily explained, and according to NASA advisors, sightings that seem to defy the limitations of current technology regarding accelerations and velocities "are scientifically interesting."

There is now a special office within the Department of Defence investigating unexplained sightings, and Congress has recently taken an interest in UFOs. For instance, a former government employee made headlines earlier this year when he informed lawmakers that alien "biologics" had been found at crash sites. However, a Pentagon spokesman claimed that the claims could not be verified.

NASA has made a point of saying that it "has not found any credible evidence of extraterrestrial life"

Eric Dawson

and that there is no proof that any observed UFOs are alien in nature.

Rather than being asked to comment on the nature of earlier unidentified observations, NASA asked the 16 researchers and other advisors who drafted recommendations to tell it what kind of data was currently available or could be obtained.

FINALLIES AND GENUINE ADVICE FROM NASA

We urge NASA to take a leading role in the entire government endeavour to understand UAP, so that it can contribute to a comprehensive, evidence-based policy based on the scientific method. We fervently request that NASA make use of its current and future Earth-observing capabilities to investigate the local environmental components linked to UAP that are first detected by other methods. By doing this, NASA may then investigate directly whether specific environmental conditions are linked to identified UAP. NASA can also look into

Eric Dawson

establishing links with the U.S. commercial remote sensing sector, which boasts robust constellations of high-resolution Earth monitoring satellites.

At the moment, UAP detection is typically accidental and is made up of sensors that lack precise data because they were not designed or calibrated for this purpose. Due to a lack of data archiving and curation, this results in a large amount of UAP whose origin is still unknown. As it is critical to detect UAP with multiple, properly calibrated sensors, we recommend NASA to use its considerable understanding in this area to potentially employ multispectral or hyperspectral data as part of an intensive data collection effort.

The panel goes on to say that in addition to meticulous data collection and careful curation, advanced data analysis techniques like machine learning and artificial intelligence need to be used in a comprehensive UAP detection campaign. Here,

Eric Dawson

we request that NASA's UAP programme be utilised for the government-wide project.

The panel believes that public engagement will be crucial to understanding UAP. NASA has already taken a step towards eradicating the stigma associated with reporting by naming UAP research after itself. Furthermore, as part of a larger effort to more systematically gather public UAP reports, we advise NASA to look into the viability of developing or acquiring a crowdsourcing system, such as open-source smartphone apps, to collect imaging data and other smartphone sensor data from numerous citizen observers.

Our final piece of advice is to correctly use the Aviation Safety Reporting System (ASRS) for commercial pilot UAP reporting, as it provides a vital database for the government's entire endeavour to comprehend UAP. The agency's longstanding relationship with the FAA would be beneficial in examining potential integrations of state-of-the-art,

Eric Dawson

real-time analytic techniques into incoming air traffic management (ATM) systems.

In summary, NASA is uniquely positioned to support its goal of advancing scientific knowledge, technical competency, and exploration by helping to conduct a thorough and methodical investigation of UAP. NASA should use its core competencies and capabilities to assess whether it should take the lead or follow suit in implementing each of the aforementioned recommendations while accounting for budgetary priorities. It is crucial to further situate NASA's involvement in relation to the larger, all-encompassing government strategy for understanding UAP.

Eric Dawson

INDIVIDUALS IN THE NASA UNIDENTIFIED ABNORMAL PHENOMENON INDEPENDENT STUDY TEAM

Chair

Dr. David Spergel

(Simons Foundation)

Designated Federal Official

Dr. Daniel Evans

(NASA IIeadquarters)

Panelists

Dr. Anamaria Berea

(George Mason University)

Eric Dawson

Dr. Federica Bianco

(University of Delaware)

Dr. Reggie Brothers

(AE Industrial Partners)

Dr. Paula Bontempi

(University of Rhode Island)

Dr. Jennifer Buss

(Potomac Institute of Policy Studies)

Dr. Nadia Drake

(Science Journalist)

Mr. Mike Gold

(Redwire Space)

Eric Dawson

Dr. David Grinspoon

(Planetary Science Institute)

Capt. Scott Kelly, USN, Ret.

(NASA Astronaut, Ret.)

Dr. Matt Mountain

(Association of Universities for Research and Astronomy)

Mr. Warren Randolph

(Federal Aviation Administration)

Dr. Walter Scott

(Maxar Technologies)

Eric Dawson

Dr. Joshua Semeter

(Boston University)

Dr. Karlin Toner

(Federal Aviation Administration)

Dr. Shelley Wright

(University of California, San Diego)

Eric Dawson